History of Russia & The Soviet Union
in Humorous Verse

By the same author

MAKE MARZIPAN, NOT WAR: Crazy Rhymes for Crazy Times
CHEESE PIRATES: Humorous Rhymes for Adult Children
CAFÉ BOMBSHELL: The International Brain Surgery Conspiracy
PETS OF THE GREAT DICTATORS & Other Works

History of Russia
& The Soviet Union
in Humorous Verse

Sabrina P. Ramet

Washington, DC

Copyright © 2014 by Sabrina P. Ramet

New Academia Publishing, 2014

All rights reserved. No part of this book may be reproduced or transmitted in any form or by any means, electronic or mechanical, including photocopying, recording, or by any information storage and retrieval system.

Printed in the United States of America

Library of Congress Control Number: 2014953595
ISBN 978-0-9906939-3-2 paperback (alk. paper)

 An imprint of new Academia Publishing
P.O. Box 27420, Washington, DC 20038-7420

 info@newacademia.com
www.newacademia.com

For Andrew Cannon

If it rhymes, it must be true.

Contents

Preface	xii
THE TSARIST ERA	1
Ivan The Terrible and his terrible goldfish	3
Fyodor The Bell-Ringer	4
Ekaterina, you're so great!	6
Peter The Great – yes, yes, yes!	8
Boris Good-Enough	9
The last of the Molokans	11
War with the Tsar of Russia	12
Twinkle, twinkle, Father Tsar	13
THE BOLSHEVIK REVOLUTION	15
C'é la Marx	17
Tired of the same old politics? Vote Bolshevik	18
Bolsheviks vs. Mensheviks	19
Lenin's cat	21
Diga diga doo, Bolsheviki	22
STALINISM & TROTSKY'S CHALLENGE	23
Stalin's spider	25
Think of Stalin	27
We all live on a great collective farm	28
In dreams I kiss the plan, madame	30
Ilya Ivanov, matchmaker	31
The assassination of Sergei Kirov	33

Humor for the masses	34
Ghost comrades in the sky	35
Trofim Lysenko – anti-geneticist with a cause	37
The origin of language	38
Who's afraid of the commissar?	39
The confiscation of saxophones, 1949	42
Hero of Socialist Labor	44
You cannot be right against the party, or Trotsky agreed with himself	45
Trotsky's rabbits	47
RUSSIA AFTER STALIN	49
Akademgorodok	51
Kazakh territory	52
The life and times of Nikita Sergeyevich Khrushchev	53
The U-2 affair	54
Gagarin looking for God	55
You are old, Comrade Brezhnev, and so is your hawk	56
These bubbles are for Brezhnev	58
The collected works of Leonid Brezhnev	60
Andropov, champion of milk drinkers	62
Rule, Chernenko!	63
Perestroika (dance version)	64
Boris Yeltsin, you know it's Boris Yeltsin!	66
Putin on the moon	67
Solipsists for Putin	69
Putin fantasizes	70
SOVIET FRIENDS ABROAD	71
Well hello, Zhivkov	73
Enver, don't shoot	74
The golden words of Mao Zedong	76

Die gute Zeiten rollen lassen	78
Ceaușescu's monkeys	80
Husak's duck	81
Ulbricht's hamsters	82
Mao's cockroach	83
Ho Chi Minh's "Parakeet"	84
Castro's speeches and his Chihuahua's comment	86
Kim Il Sung's fellow traveler	88
Tito and his self-managing goat	90
Kadar's pedigree Pooch	92
Riding High with Enver Hoxha	94
Gomulka's Aardvark	96
Gierek the leader & Melsor the toad	98

Preface

The verses herein are inspired by actual historical personalities, events, and eras, but, although some of what is recalled here is factually accurate, some of it is not and, even those portions which may be roughly true to history, are – I suppose – presented in an unfamiliar way. Some of these verses recall some strange times, such as Tsar Fyodor's obsession with bells or Ilya Ivanov's experiments with animal hybridization. It is not my purpose to suggest that such things were unique to the Soviet Union or to Russia. Quite on the contrary, one may find strange and bizarre personalities, events, and episodes in probably every country in the world. Indeed, I have celebrated strange and bizarre elements in American and French history in my *Cheese Pirates,* British, Libyan, Spanish, and ancient Roman leaders in my *Pets of the Great Dictators,* and some oddities of American, British, Libyan, and Yugoslav history and politics in my *Make Marzipan, Not War.* It is my hope that this collection will afford some amusement to both those who already know something about Russian and Soviet history and those who do not, and that it may inspire some with little familiarity with Soviet history to want to explore that subject in a serious way.

Most of the verses included herein, were published previously in my collections, *Pets of the Great Dictators* (2006; 2nd ed., 2008), *Cheese Pirates: Humorous rhymes for adult children* (2010), and *Make Marzipan, Not War: Crazy rhymes for crazy times* (2013), all published by Scarith Books, a division of New Academia Publishing. I am grateful to Anna Lawton, my publisher, for permission to collect these verses in a new collection. The following verses appear for the first time in this collection: "Fyodor the bell ringer", "Ekaterina, you're so great!", "Peter the Great – yes, yes, yes!", "Boris Good-Enough", "Diga diga doo, Bolsheviki!", "In dreams I kiss the plan, madame", "Ilya Ivanov, matchmaker", "The assassination of Sergei Kirov", "The origin of language", "Who's afraid of the commissar?", "The confiscation of saxophones, 1949", "Kazakh territory", "The life and times of Nikita Sergeyevich Khrushchev", "The U-2 affair", "These bubbles are for Brezhnev", "The collected works of Leonid Brezhnev", "Andropov, champion of milk drinkers", "Rule, Chernenko!", "Boris Yeltsin, you know it's Boris Yeltsin!", "Perestroika (dance version)", "Solipsists for Putin", and "Putin fantasizes".

The art appearing on page 58 was prepared by Ingrid Rosenvinge. All other art was provided by Christine M. Hassenstab.

Sabrina P. Ramet

THE TSARIST ERA

Ivan The Terrible and his terrible goldfish

(Composed sometime between 1997 and early 2003)

I've never seen a fish laugh,
At least not very loudly,
said Ivan the Terrible to himself,
as he gazed in the mirror proudly.

I've never seen a goldfish smile
Hey diddle diddle for the Oprichnina,
Maybe that's just not their style,
Hey diddle diddle for the Oprichnina.

My little fish must be a priest,
It likes to sing in chant.
But that terrible fish always sings off key --
which is why it must stay in the tank.

Bash them, smash them, and give them the lash,
Hey diddle diddle for the Oprichnina,
All of my enemies gonna crash,
Hey diddle diddle for the Oprichnina.

Fyodor The Bell-Ringer

(Composed on 12 April 2014, between 1:50 and 2:18 a.m., during a short break from my slumber)

Fyodor Ivanovich, he was tsar,
he heard bells from near and far –
big bells, small bells, tiny little tinkle bells,
listened to bells in his boudoir.
With a ring-a-ding ding, and a ring-a-ding dong,
ring-a-ding, ring-a-dong all day long.

Policy-making was a bore:
he told his ministers to attend to that chore,
big bells, small bells, tiny little tinkle bells,
that was the sound he could adore.
With a ring-a-ding ding, and a ring-a-ding dong,
he liked to hear bells all day long.

Off to the chapel he would spring,
they had bells that he could ring:
big bells, small bells, tiny little tinkle bells,
did as he liked 'cause he was king.
With a ring-a-ding ding, and a ring-a-ding dong,
he could ring bells all day long.

Sometimes he would like to kneel,
his courtiers played the glockenspiel,
big bells, small bells, tiny little tinkle bells,
and back to bells with renewed zeal.
With a ring-a-ding ding, and a ring-a-ding dong,
ring-a-ding, ring-a-dong all day long.

Ekaterina, you're so great!

(Composed to the tune of "Der Trommelmann" on 6 April 2014, between 4:30 and 4:41 a.m. I had trouble sleeping.)

Ekaterina – ja,
pa-rampa-pa-pa
she was the ruler – da,
pa-rampa-pa-pa
she had some lovers – si,
pa-rampa-pa-pa
she left them happy – yes,
pa-rampa-pa-pa, rampa-pa-pa, rampa-pa-pa.

She, the Empress – oui,
pa-rampa-pa-pa
she annexed Poland – po
pa-rampa-pa-pa,
but no, not all of it,
pa-rampa-pa-pa
she shared it with some friends
pa-rampa-pa-pa, rampa-pa-pa, rampa-pa-pa.

Now the whole world says,
pa-rampa-pa-pa
that she was really great
pa-rampa-pa-pa
and surely you agree
pa-rampa-pa-pa
and surely you agree,
pa-rampa-pa-pa, rampa-pa-pa, rampa-pa-pa,
Rampa-pa-pa!!

Peter The Great - yes, yes, yes!

(Composed on 6 April 2014, at 8:30 a.m., soon after waking up)

When you reflect on Peter the Great, what always comes to mind?
Is it the fact he hated beards, it is the fact that he was kind?
Peter the Great never was late – no, no, no!
Constructed his city over the dead, buried down below.
Peter the Great liked building ships – yes, yes, yes!
Where did he go to learn that trade? – guess, guess, guess!
The Netherlands, of course my dear – smart, smart, smart!
That is the place to learn that art – art, art, art!
Peter the Great never was late – no, no, no!
Constructed his city over the dead, buried down below.

Boris Good-Enough

(Composed in April 2014)

Much loved he'd been the first years of his reign –
opening schools, he was using his brain.
Lutherans gained his permission to open
churches in Russia, and others were hopin'
that his tolerant policies would be continued –
he was a tsar both kind-hearted and shrewd.
But when he fell ill, people thought it a curse,
Convinced that their lives could only get worse.

Boris was gentle and quite good enough,
wise when he saw that the folk had it rough,
told all his courtiers to distribute some cash
to the people, but no, they just wanted the lash:
"Beat us and treat us like slaves to your throne,
then back to your palace and leave us alone."

He saw that the people had nothing to eat,
so his courtiers distributed food on the street,
but people refused it, it just wasn't right
that Boris the tsar was concerned 'bout their plight,
and people complained that the tsar was too meek
and that his credentials to rule them were weak.

But things did get worse, with the great Times of Troubles,
from one day to the next complaints would be doubled.
Famine and pestilence swept through the land,
the boyars now wanted to take things in hand.
Three False Dimitrys rose from the dead,
each wanting to rule as Great Russia's head.

The Poles had an army and sent it along,
the Russians then realized that something was wrong.

The nation then rose and threw out the Poles,
along with their recipes, forks, plates, and bowls.
"Russians must eat as Russians must eat!" –
that was a slogan that no one could beat!
And thus came a Romanov, Mikhail, to rule –
here was a tsar whom no one could fool.
And Russian continued with tsars for a while,
with Romanovs marching all in a file.

The last of the Molokans

(Composed in Tartu on 20 May 2012)

The last of the Molokans – they're drinking all the milk.
They know that all those vitamins are good for all their ilk.
They're drinking milk at night, they're drinking milk at noon,
they pour a little cocoa in and stir it with a spoon.
They dip a biscuit in it, and swirl it all around,
they drink their milk while standing or while sitting on the ground.
And when they're feeling happy – or so I've heard it said –
they try to drink a round of milk, each standing on his head.

War with the Tsar of Russia

(Composed sometime between June 2007 and June 2010)

In seventeen hundred and sixty-eight
The Sultan Mustafa could no longer wait,
So he sent his troops out through Istanbul's gate
For a war with the tsar of Russia.

He thought an alliance with Poles would serve
To boost the morale of his men and unnerve
The Russians who'd sworn to always observe
The decrees of the tsar of Russia.

But Suvurov defeated the Poles on land
While at sea too the Turkish fleet could not withstand
The fleet under Admiral Orlov's command
Who brought triumph to the tsar of Russia.

The Russians and Turks signed a treaty of peace
Which called for the combat and fighting to cease
With Crimea assigned to the Russians on lease,
For His Highness the tsar of Russia.

Twinke twinkle, Father Tsar

(Composed sometime between June 2007 and June 2010)

Twinkle twinkle, Father Tsar,
your Rasputin is bizarre
mystic healer or a drunk,
who knows the depths to which he'd sunk?
But in the stories that were spun,
it seems he helped the prince, your son.

While the Bolshies made their plot,
you sailed around, enjoyed your yacht.
Lenin, Trotsky, and their lot
took you for an idiot.
But you ruled quite absolute –
you were a man of known repute.

Twinkle twinkle, Father Tsar,
how I wonder what you are,
high above the world you hide,
by your people deified.
But all things come to an end,
and that's a law you don't transcend.

Twinkle twinkle, Father Tsar,
how I wonder what you are.

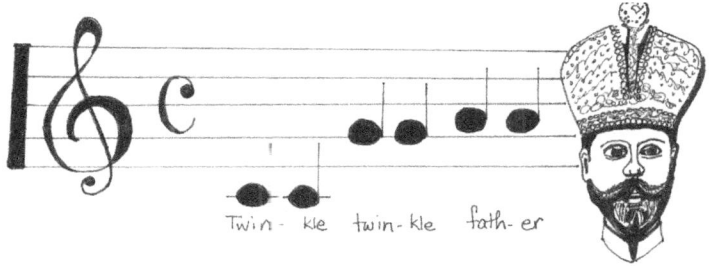

THE BOLSHEVIK REVOLUTION

C'é la Marx

(Inspired, roughly, by the tune of "C'é la luna", a song popularized by Louis Prima. Composed sometime between 2002 and early 2005)

No no no no, it never is too late,
no no no, to overthrow the state
no no no, 'cause it's capitalism's mate,
no no no, exploitation's not our fate.

Marx and Engels wanted more
and to open up the door
for a better life for workers,
Why give profits to the shirkers
just because they own the store?

No no no no, it never is too late,
no no no, to overthrow the state
no no no, 'cause it's capitalism's mate,
no no no, exploitation's not our fate.

Hey! the system's bad – alas!
Inequalities of class –
and they make our stomachs growl.
Exploitation is so foul
that I hope it cannot last,
I feel so alienated that I always gotta sing…

No no no no, it never is too late
no no no, to overthrow the state
no no no, 'cause it's capitalism's mate,
no no no, exploitation's not our fate!

Tired of the same old politics? Vote Bolshevik

(Composed on 11/12 March 2011. If you can't guess the tune, you're no Bolshevik!)

If you believe the rich should rule
and treat the citizens as dopes,
then, comrade, you are quite a fool
and you've given up all hope.
But the Bolsheviks are not the same
as the exploiters whom you know,
they light the revolution's flame
and then they make our spirits glow.
While the rich folks have stolen
from the workers and the tramps,
the Bolsheviks will change all this
and put the rich in camps.
If you're tired of the way
politicians have behaved,
then vote for Bolsheviks today --
you'll see: they're all the rave!

Bolshevik vs. Menshevik

(Composed sometime between June 2007 and June 2010. May be sung to the tune of "Davey Crockett, King of the Wild Frontier")

Vladimir Lenin was the workers' friend
he worked very hard to the bitter end
he spared no effort to make himself heard
his political vision – it was never blurred.
Lenin, Lenin and Trotsky
Kings of the Bolsheviks!

His plan was the biggest, his plan was the best
to take over Russia from the east to the west
"Peace, land, bread" and Kerensky out!
Every revolution means that people gonna shout.
Lenin, Lenin and Trotsky
Kings of the Bolsheviks!

But the Russian Social Democrats needed to meet
'cause their disagreements were not so discreet
Axelrod, Zasulich, Potresov too
agreed with bearded Martov and all of his crew.
Lenin, Lenin and Trotsky
Kings of the Bolsheviks!

Now Julius Martov was a Menshevik,
his whole approach made Lenin sick
he thought that anyone who came through the door
ought to be admitted to the party's inner corps.
Lenin, Lenin and Trotsky
Kings of the Bolsheviks!

But Lenin and Trotsky both knew that

you couldn't run a party with a welcome mat,
makin' revolution was a tricky case,
So cadres in the party had to show a common face.
Lenin, Lenin and Trotsky
Kings of the Bolsheviks!

So Trotsky told the Mensheviks that they could go
to the dustbin of history and join the tableau
of bankrupt lackeys who didn't have a clue
and frenzied exploiters who were really through.
Lenin, Lenin and Trotsky
Kings of the Bolsheviks!

Now Lenin and Trotsky and the Bolshevik team
worked to overthrow the old regime,
they seized the power from behind the scene
and were feted and cheered wherever they were seen.
Lenin, Lenin and Trotsky
Kings of the Bolsheviks!
Lenin, Lenin and Trotsky
Kings of the Bolsheviks!

Lenin's cat

(Composed in April 2006)

Lenin wasn't born a communist
And nor was his cat.
He wasn't born a leader
And nor was his cat.

He spent some time in Switzerland
Planning revolution.
He knew that seizing power was
The optimal solution.

He liked to stroke his little pet
And comb its pretty fur
He liked to smoke a cigarette
And hear his kitty purr.

He liked to ride on well-sealed trains
And organized a party.
Everyone's invited but
To join you should be hearty.

Diga diga doo, Bolsheviki

(Composed on 15—16 April 2014)

Stalin thought that jazz was bad,
thought it was a bourgeois fad
diga diga doo Bolsheviki, diga diga doo Bolshevik!
Voroshilov disagreed,
liked to dance and liked to lead
diga diga doo Bolsheviki, diga diga doo Bolshevik!

I'm so really very Bolshevik by nature,
if you don't shout "Down with Trotsky's legions!",
you're gonna lose your pop!
So, let those funny Mensheviks
and Trotskyites go play with sticks,
diga diga doo Bolsheviki, diga diga doo Bolshevik!

STALINISM AND TROTSKY'S CHALLENGE

Stalin's Spider

(Composed sometime between 1997 and 2003. With apologies to "Little Miss Muffet" and to Christopher Marlowe)

Comrade Joe Stalin
sat on a victim
eating his curds and wey,
when along came a spider
and sat down beside her,
as it began to say,
"You are so very big
And your hair is dark and bushy,
I think I'll rest in your moustache,
I'm sure that would be cushy."
Said Stalin to the spider,
as it crawled onto his knee,
"Come live with me and be my love
and we shall all the pleasures prove
that webs and traps and show trials proffer --
All of that and more I offer.
There we shall trap both friend and kin,
accusing them of every sin,
constrain them to confess to all,
For broken men sing madrigals.
I too weave webs to trap my foes
and lure them to their dooms,
but unlike you I guarantee
to lay them in their tombs.
There's no advantage, spider-friend,
in messing up the house,
with carcasses of every louse,
who's met his timely end.
And I shall make thee webs of notions:

propaganda -- that's my style.
Fill your head with wondrous fancies --
All of this but for your smile."
And so they lived together,
like two birds of a feather --
the spider weaving webs of silk,
and Stalin webs of lies.
For spiders do not trap their ilk
they're only after bugs,
but Stalin put them all away,
accused of being thugs.
The spider's life was short but happy,
Stalin's life was long,
But neither ever suffered doubts
or feared he had done wrong.

Think of Stalin

(Composed in 2010)

When you lie awake at night and you find you cannot sleep
(just) think about the Five-Year Plan and Russia's giant forward leap.
When, at parties, making friends, what to talk about you ask –
why not talk of Stalin's thoughts and about the people's task?
Then at dinner, at your home, while you ingest food,
you can talk of Trotsky and his anti-Soviet brood.
After dinner, in your bed, talk of Stalin with your wife,
this can but excite you both: just think of Stalin all your life.

We all live on a great collective farm

[This text has been approved by the Central Committee of the Center for Poetry, Song, and Unwinding (CPSU) for use, on a voluntary basis, at all CPSU functions. It is not mandatory, under the current Five Year Plan, to sing it to the tune of the Beatles' "We all live in a yellow submarine", but monitor CPSU bulletins for updates under the next Five Year Plan. Composed in 2010]

On our great collective farm
we love working dawn to gloam,
all our lands were communized –
so the kolkhoz is also home.

We like writing our reports
which the party always reads,
and we always work the plan,
'til a new one supersedes.

We all live on a great collective farm,
a great collective farm, a great collective farm,
we all live on a great collective farm,
it really has its charm, the great collective farm.

What we plant – it has been planned
by the wisest of humankind,
all the knowledge of our land
has been poured into planners' minds.

Down at GOSPLAN they know all,
which is why ther're no mistakes,
and if you think there were mistakes,
you belong with Trotsky's snakes.

GOSPLAN knows what we ought to plant and sow,
we ought to plant and sow, we ought to plant and sow,
GOSPLAN knows what we ought to plant and sow,
it's good that they foreknow what we ought to plant and sow.

MTS has chaser bins
it has tractors and swathers too,
it has harrows and yellow balers,
it has everything for me and you.

We don't need to own our tools,
we don't need equipment – no!
MTS is all we need,
The party tells us and so we know.

We all live on a great collective farm,
a great collective farm, a great collective farm,
we all live on a great collective farm,
it really has its charm, the great collective farm.

In dreams I kiss the plan, madame

(Composed on 25 April 2014; may be sung to the melody of "In dreams I kiss your hand, madame", Vic Damone wrote the lyrics to the original version, which was sung by Bing Crosby and Vaughn Monroe, among others.)

In dreams I kiss the plan, madame,
I'm dizzy with success.
My grindstone to the nose, madame,
I'm cleaning up the mess.
My many hands make work, madame,
I'm ready to confess.
My tractor is my spouse, madame,
I thought you'd never guess.

Ilya Ivanov, matchmaker

(Composed on 23—25 April 2014. Inspired by Udo Lindenberg's 1983 hit, "Sonderzug nach Pankow", which was in turn inspired by Harry Warren's 1941 hit, "Chattanooga Choo Choo", famously performed by Glenn Miller and his orchestra.)

Pardon me please, is this the railway to the future?
I have lots of ideas
and I know they will please.
I want to work
with the super minds of Russia,
the best that we have.
I want to play in that band.

Ilya Ivanov was a scientist of note,
working for the Kremlin in a white cotton coat,
Ilya was a breeder
Stalin was his leader:
making hybrid species was the writ of the day.

Introduced a zebra to a donkey one day,
they got along and brought along a zonkey – hurray!
Ilya had some notions,
made a big commotion
to prove that making hybrids was a Marxist idea.

Comrades agree, we're on the railway to the future:
everyone's glad
because the system is good.
I love to work
on the Five-Year Plan,
I'm a bit dizzy now –
I want to work on the Plan.

Cross a turtle with a bird – a burtle you get,

cross a lizard with a snake – a snizard you get,
riding on a cramel, stroking down a szadger,
mixing up the animals is progress now!

Ivanov was sure, he could inseminate a chimp
with the sperm of a man,
but it just wouldn't take.
He planned the reverse,
and even had a volunteer,
til Stalin put him, Stalin put him, Stalin put him in the Gulag.

Whoo whoo!

The assassination of Sergei Kirov

(May be sung to the tune of "Me and my shadow", a 1927 song written by Billy Rose and Dave Dreyer, performed among many others by "Whispering" Jack Smith and Perry Como, as well as by Bob Newhart and Peter Bonerz in one of the episodes of the 1970s sit-com, "The Bob Newhart Show". Composed in April 2014)

Just Nikolayev
walkin' up the avenue,
he had a pistol,
wanted to kill Comrade Kirov now.

And no, he never knocked,
the trigger cocked,
he strolled right in,
gave Kirov a spin.

Just Nikolayev,
all alone and feelin' red.

But then they hauled him in,
he should confess:
that Kamenev,
he gave him ideas.

Hey, just Nikolayev
all alone and all too blue.

Humor for the masses

(Composed on 29 September 2010)

Here at the People's Combine for the Production of Merriment
we make jokes.
Yes comrades -- and we do it for you!
Because, in a people's state,
it is the people who laugh,
while in a capitalistic state,
it is the capitalists who laugh.

So we make jokes for the people,
we poke fun at greedy capitalists
(in foreign countries)
and frenzied exploiters
(also in foreign countries).
We expose the insidious lies
in capitalistic jokes,
and the cryptic messages in imperialist jokes
designed to enslave you.

Yes comrades: we are on your side!
When we make a joke,
only the capitalists and imperialists cringe
and beg for mercy.
We want you to be merry.
That's why
here at the People's Combine for the Production of Merriment
we make jokes.

Ghost comrades in the sky

(Composed on 27 and 29 January 2011; inspired by the song "Ghost Riders in the Sky", written on 5 June 1948 by Stan Jones)

The comrades at the factory were making marzi-PAN,
and talking 'bout how they could best fulfill the Five Year Plan,
when all at once a shout was heard and there were verbal sparks
of genuine excitement at the mention of Karl Marx.

Yippie-yi-yay, yippie-yi-yo
Marzipan comrades work the plan!

Their fingernails were dirty, they were filled with marzi-PAN,
and beads of sweat were building up on each and every man.
They thought about Bukharin and sometimes Stalin too,
and hoped to be the fastest and the most efficient crew.

Yippie-yi-yay, yippie-yi-yo
Marzipan comrades work the plan!

And as the work-day ended, they looked up in the sky
and saw the ghosts of fallen comrades, heard their mournful cry.
They'd failed to meet the targets; just listen as they sigh,
"We've got to work forever in the collective in the sky."

Yippie-yi-yay, yippe-yi-yo
Ghost comrades in the sky!

They'd been accused of sabotage: they'd failed to reach the goal,
they then were liquidated and thrown into a hole.
Their minds had been polluted by anti-party thoughts,
in the act of not believing the party they'd been caught.

Yippie-yi-yay, yippie-yi-yo
Ghost comrades in the sky!

As the comrade-ghosts kept working, they shouted down below,
"Forget the things you've learned in school and what you think you know.
The only thing you need to know is that the party's right,
Remember that forever and keep the plan in sight."

Yippie-yi-yay, yippie-yi-yo
Ghost comrades in the sky!

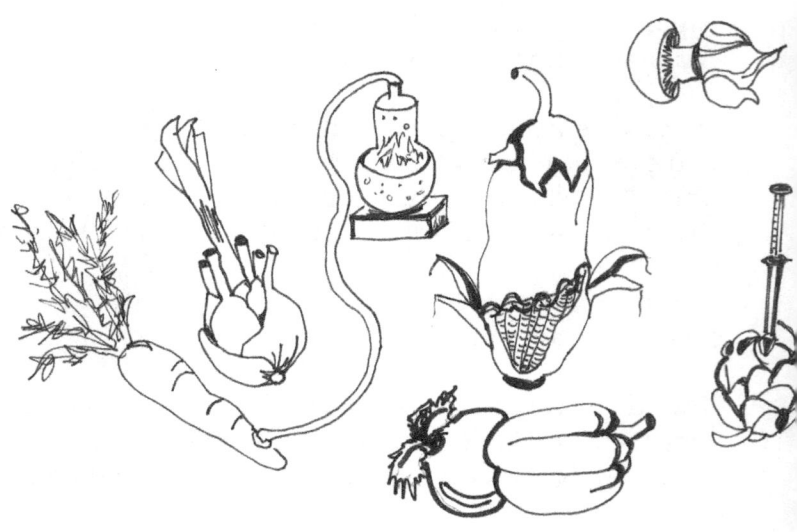

Trofim Lysenko - antigeneticist with a cause

(Composed sometime between June 2007 and June 2010, recalling the exploits of the Soviet Union's most (in)famous antigeneticist)

Everybody knows that I am what you see
I can make a carrot grow as big as a tree
I can make a cantaloupe that fills up the sea
It's time that you admit that you're indebted to me.

Give me a prize
for vegetable size
Give me a toot
for the size of your fruit.

Trofim Lysenko – that is my name
Making crops grow bigger is the name of the game
Genetics is a lie, you can be what you will
Down with Charlie Darwin 'cause he's over the hill.

Give me a toast
just let me boast
Of all of my deeds
and for meeting your needs.

Everybody knows …. La – la – la
Trofim Lysenko …. La – la – la
Down with genetics …. La – la – la
Crops growing bigger …. La – la – la
La – la – la, la – la – la.
Trofim Lysenko – that is my name!

The origin of language

(Composed on 17 April 2014.)

Nikolai Marr, the "linguist", found
there were just four original sounds.
When primitive people sat around,
their language consisted of these four sounds:
sal, ber, jon, and rosh –
they couldn't say poo or pish or bosh.
I'm no linguist, but I'd guess
that "salber" meant exactly "yes",
"jonrosh" may have been used for "no"
and "salrosh" for "it might be so."
Of other linguists, Marr was leary,
since they didn't buy his theory,
but they ended up in dungeons
while Marr was toasted at gala luncheons.

Who's afraid of the commissar?

(In February 1948, Andrei Zhdanov, member of the Politburo and Soviet cultural tsar since 1946, summoned Sergei Prokofiev, Dmitry Shostakovich, Aram Khachaturian, Dimitry Kabalevsky, and Nikolai Miaskovsky to a meeting. Instead of praising them for their symphonies, ballets, and musical suites, he dressed these prominent composers down for "formalism" and for writing music out of touch with the Soviet masses. This resulted in the cancelation of commissions and concert contracts for the five affected composers. This rendition of that sad episode was composed on 7 May 2014 in the car, while driving from Saginaw (Michigan) to Ann Arbor and listening to Max Raabe's rendition, with the Palast Orchester, of "Who's afraid of the big bad wolf". I revised my text in Hundhamaren on 15 May. The music was written by Frank Churchill, and the original lyrics – not the lyrics presented here – were written by Frank Churchill and Ann Ronell. The song was featured in the 1933 Disney film, "Three Little Pigs" and was one of the top hits of the 1930s.)

Who's afraid of the commissar, the commissar, the commissar?
Who's afraid of the commissar? Tra la la la la.
(Whistle the tune from the foregoing two lines.)

Long ago there were three men,
great composers – yes they were.
For the big but very big commissar
they did not give three figs!

Old Prokofiev thought he'd try,
to write a piece to satisfy:
if you quote from Marx,
there'll be no sparks,
but he was hung to dry!

But Kabalevsky thought
that comedians were the best,
so he wrote a suite

with a gallop too,
and put it to the test.
And Shostakovich was
the third man in this group:
he buried his thoughts
in a murky code
that no one understood.

Ha ha ha! The two other
musical men just cringed but laughed. Ha ha ha!

Who's afraid of the commissar, the commissar, the commissar?
Who's afraid of the commissar? Tra la la la la.

But things went upside down,
when Zhdanov came to town.
With a gruff complaint, when he heard a taint
and Prokofiev fell right down.

Kabalevsky took to fright,
of the big bad Zhdanov's might:
"Music's not for fun --
so says our number one" –
and Kabalevsky caved.

Shostakovich was the last,
except for two not mentioned here –
though he was a genius,
he too felt a stroke of fear:
concerts canceled, contracts nixed,
these were two of Zhdanov's tricks.

Ha ha ha!
The big but very bad commissar just laughed!
Ha ha ha ha ha!

Who's afraid of the commissar, the commissar, the commissar?
Who's afraid of the commissar? Tra la la la la.
(Whistle the tune from the foregoing two lines.)

The confiscation of saxophones, 1949

(*I read S. Frederick Starr's brilliant classic,* Red and Hot: The fate of jazz in the Soviet Union, *many years ago, but reread the section on the Stalin years in April 2014. Starr's account of the confiscation of saxophones struck me on second reading, and this verse celebrates that strange chapter in the Stalin era. Verse composed on 27—28 April 2014; I set it to the tune of "When Johnny Comes Marching Home Again" because I thought that that jolly march would capture the "wisdom" of this campaign perfectly.*)

We confiscate the saxophones – hurrah, hurrah!
You won't be needing gramophones – hurrah, hurrah!
Our comrade leader understands
the threat that's posed by dance hall bands,
so we hope you'll switch to playing the bassoon.

A dark bassoon's a better choice – hurrah, hurrah!
This is a time you can rejoice – hurrah, hurrah!
Whatever our vozhd has figured out,
you know he's right without a doubt,
so obey and just don't ask what it's about.

We confiscate the saxophones – hurrah, hurrah!
You won't be needing gramophones – hurrah, hurrah!
Our comrade leader understands
the threat that's posed by dance hall bands,
so we hope you'll switch to playing the bassoon.

Hero of Socialist Labor

(Composed sometime between June 2007 and June 2010)

I can mine a hundred tons of coal per shift
I've got muscle and there's tons that I can lift
My hero is Stakhanov
He's obviously a one-off
I can mine a hundred tons of coal per shift.

Aleksei Stakhanov mined a hundred eight
Back in 1935 he pulled his weight
My hero is Stakhanov
He's obviously a one-off
Aleksei Stakhanov mined a hundred eight.

He set records that will stand the test of time
And he did it when no longer in his prime
Hey, my hero is Stakhanov
He's obviously a one-off
He set records that will stand the test of time.

You cannot be right against the party, or Trotsky agreed with himself

(Composed on 27—28 August 2010)

It's clear that if the party's right
and you don't agree
that you are clearly in the wrong
and don't think that you're free,
'cause freedom means that you are right
and not to be in error,
to choose to stay in ignorance
is self-inflicted terror.
You cannot be right
you cannot be right
against the party, no

This insight came from Trotsky,
before he lost to Koba,
At least he didn't lose his teeth,
for that he thanked his zubar.
But once he'd lost to Stalin
ole Trotsky said the key
would be to make another party
with which he could agree.
You cannot be right
you cannot be right
against the party, no!

An International was what
was needed all around,
it would be number 4 because
the Third had run aground.

And if he ran the party, well,
he knew he would agree
with everything the party said,
the slogan would still be:
You cannot be right
you cannot be right
against the party, no!

Trotsky's rabbit

(Composed on 18 November 2010)

Trotsky had some rabbits
he kept in a pen,
they had such tempered habits
that he always said of them:
"These, my rabbits,
they're loyal and true,
they'd never cater
to Stalin's crew."

The rabbits had a system
to meet each rabbit's needs:
decisions in committees
allocating feeds.
The rabbits had
self-management –
firm foundation
like cement.

When it came to irrigation,
it should be permanent –
so said all Trotsky's rabbits
and that is what they meant.
His rabbits knew
to get good crops
you've got to irrigate
the land a lot.

So the cry went out
from Trotsky's rabbits:
"Permanent irritation
and tempered habits!
and when we prey on lettuce
and lettuce is our prey,
we often like to sing and say –
time for dinner, lettuce prey!"

RUSSIA AFTER STALIN

Akademgorodok

(Composed on 16 November 2011)

Academic City – books are us!

We have a drive-in library, you sit inside your car
and read the works of Brezhnev on the giant screen afar.

Our restaurants are popular, the waiters can recite
the items on the menu and serve them through the night.

They also know their Chekhov and Dostoyevsky too
and can recite from memory *War and Peace,* Part Two.

Our research is important, we're hoping to devise
a way to undo global warming: that would be so wise.

We're looking to the future, and want to end all war:
we know you'll be delighted with what we have in store.

Our youngsters – when they go on dates – they take just what they'll need:
and take along some works of science – there's just so much to read.

So, next time you're in Russia and looking for your nook,
come visit us in Akademgorodok and find yourself a book.

Academic City – books are us!

Kazakh territory

(May be sung to the tune of the theme song to "Tombstone Territory", an American Western series starring Pat Conway and Richard Eastham, which aired on television 1957—59, with reruns during 1960. Composed on 21 April 2014, this verse recalls the fate suffered by Georgi Malenkov and Lazar Kaganovich, members of the so-called "anti-party group", when they failed to oust Nikita Khrushchev in 1957.)

Whistle me Georgi Malenkov
Whistle him out to Kazakhstan
Whistle him a job to run a plant in Kazakh territory.

Since he had run against Khrushchev,
that was where he had to be,
and Kaganovich was director withal
of a new cement factory.

Whistle me Georgi Malenkov
Whistle him out to Kazakhstan
Whistle him a job to run a plant in Kazakh territory.

The life and times of Nikita Sergeyevich Khrushschev

(Composed on 14 March 2014, on a KLM flight from Amsterdam to Trondheim. This may be sung to the tune of "Hokey Pokey", a song possibly written by Al Tabor, a British band leader, in 1940.)

(1957)
It's Comrade Khrushchev in,
Comrade Khrushchev out,
Comrade Khrushchev in
and you twirl him all about,
the anti-party groupies surely made a lot of noise –
that's what it's all about!

(1962)
He put the missiles in,
he took the missiles out,
he put the missiles in
and he twirled them all about,
the USA got nervous and it made a lot of noise –
that's what it's all about!

(1964)
Comrade Brezhnev said,
Comrade Suslov said,
and Podgorny said
that he really should retire.
But Khrushchev wrote his memoirs and he twirled them all about–
that's what it's all about!

The U-2 affair

(Composed on 14 November 2014, between 4:29 and 4:46 a.m.)

Dwight D. Eisenhower -- what a pretty name!
He was president and when his duck was lame,
he sent up an airplane to do a little spying --
how pretty it was, as long as it was flying.

U-2, U-2, take lot of pics,
U-2, U-2, yes we're full of tricks.

The airplane flew so very very high,
Captain Powers, pilot, made such a handsome spy,
but flying over Russia, it had a little crash
and fell to the ground with a boom and a bash.

U-2, U-2, take a lot of pics,
U-2, U-2, yes we're full of tricks.

Old man Khrushchev, now he was accusing
the West of doing some spying and abusing
of Russian airspace -- which the White House just denied,
and Eisenhower sat before the camera and he lied.

U-2, U-2, take a lot of pics,
U-2, U-2, yes we're full of tricks.

But this warn't smart, 'cause Khrushchev had the proof
and he marched out Powers and made him utter "woof".
Now there was pudding on Eisenhower's face,
and spy-masters everywhere'd been put in their place.

U-2, U-2, take a lot of pics,
U-2, U-2, yes we're full of tricks.

Gagarin looking for God

(Composed on 21 April 2014; may be sung to the tune of "Getting to Know You", as featured in the film, "The King and I", a musical created by Richard Rodgers and Oscar Hammerstein II. The story that Gagarin announced that he could not find God in space is now often held to have been apocryphal.)

Yuri Gagarin
looking for God all around him,
flew out to space
hoping to see God out there.

Yuri Gagarin
training in Sochi –
effective.
He was precisely
the best of all.

Yuri Gagarin –
he was a cosmonaut and flying,
getting to like space,
getting to hope space liked him.

Yuri Gagarin
couldn't find God
in space.
Came back a hero –
the best of all.

You are old, Comrade Brezhnev, and so is your hawk

(Composed sometime between 2002 and early 2006)

"You are old Comrade Brezhnev," the young pioneer said,
"and your muscles are no longer limber,
But you toss around logs as if they were nothing.
Pray how do you lift all this timber?"

"In my youth," said Leonid Ilych, "in the communist league,
I recited the *Eighteenth Brumaire*
For hours on end, 'til I had it by heart.
After that, logs seem lighter than air."

"You are old, Comrade Brezhnev," the young pioneer said,
"and you've grown most conspicuously fat,
But you locked up ten dissidents in five seconds flat.
Pray, sir, how can *you* manage that?"

"In my youth," said Leonid Ilych, "I'd often denounce
All the capitalists who tried to repress us.
I grew so adept that it's nothing at all
To imprison these scum who depress us."

"You are old, Comrade Brezhnev," the young pioneer said,
"And your mind is essentially dead.
Yet you've trained a pet hawk how to handle your car.
Pray, how did you manage to train her that far?"

"In my youth I commanded a squadron of tanks,"
said Leonid Ilych, improving the story.
"With my hawk at my side I defended my flanks
and pushed onward to triumph and glory.

Since then I have shared every trick of the trade
with my pet hawk who sits at my side.
So what's the surprise if after these years,
my hawk takes me out for a ride?"

"You are old, Comrade Brezhnev, and so is your hawk,
And all of the Politburo as well.
Yet your hawk's writing her memoirs and you've written yours.
Pray, why do you make our lives hell?"

"I have listened in patience to all of your prattle,
and have answered three questions of yours.
Now out of my sight or I'll throw you in jail
and I'll make sure to twice-bolt the doors."

These bubbles are for Brezhnev

(Completed on 3 June 2014. This verse may be sung to the tune of "Mein kleiner grüner Kaktus", a song first popularized by the Comedian Harmonists, a male choral ensemble active in Berlin in the years 1929-34, and revived more recently by Max Raabe and the Palast Orchester.)

Es bringt ihm Freude an Volk zu schauen,
als sie das Kommunismus bauen.
Brezhnev mag Autos, damit zu fahren
und Sozialismus zu bewahren!

These bubbles are for Brezhnev, we're blowing them with joy -
hollari, hollari, hollaro!
We like him as a comrade, we liked him as a boy –
hollari, hollari, hollaro!
Kagda my khatim pit', ne mozhem podazhdat',
My vsegda vybirayem malaka, -ka, -ka!
These bubbles are for Brezhnev, we're blowing them with joy!
Hollari, hollari, hollaro!

Hat eine Katze, die passt auf die Ratse,
die beide denken an die Zukunft!
Er braucht nicht zu eilen, mit so viele Medaillen,
so sitzt er und denkt an den Lenin.

Nam nravitsa partiinost',
nam nravitsa zastoy!
Hollari, hollari, hollaro!
Ya lyublyu Suslova,
Podgornogo tak-tak,
Hollari, hollari, hollaro!

Nash Brezhnev ne Zinoviev
i tozhe ne Trotsky,

i pravda – vsegda pravda dazhe po subbotam.
I nakoniets my skazhem do svidaniya zdes' –
Hollari, hollari, hollaro!

Translation:

It brings him joy to watch the people,
as they build socialism.
Brezhnev likes cars, so that he can drive
and preserve socialism!

These bubbles are for Brezhnev, we're blowing them with joy –
hollari, hollari, hollaro!
We like him as a comrade, we liked him as a boy –
hollari, hollari, hollaro!
When we want to drink, no no we cannot wait,
We're always choosing milk, milk, milk!
These bubbles are for Brezhnev, we're blowing them with joy!
Hollari, hollari, hollaro!

He has a cat, that takes care of the rat,
both of them think about the future!
He doesn't need to rush, with so many medals.
So he sits and thinks about Lenin.

Party-mindedness pleases us,
stagnation pleases us!
I love Suslov,
Podgorny so-so,
Hollari, hollari, hollaro!

Our Brezhnev is no Zinoviev,
and Trotsky also not,
and truth is always truth, even on Saturdays.
And finally we say goodbye here!
Hollari, hollari, hollaro!

The collected works of Leonid Brezhnev

(Composed in Ann Arbor in the Sheraton Hotel, Room 608, in the evening of 7 May 2014. This should be sung to the tune of "Hi ho, hi ho, it's home from work we go", from the Walt Disney film, "Snow White and the Seven Dwarfs".)

Hi ho, hi ho!
Hi ho, hi ho, we're reading Brezhnev's works,
we're loving volumes 1 through 8,
hi ho, hi ho, hi ho,
hi ho, hi ho, we haven't finished yet,
there're 7 volumes more – you bet!
Hi ho, hi ho, hi ho!

We read read read read read read read read read all of Brezhnev's works!
We like especially volume 8 – in fact, we've read it twice!

It ain't no trick
to get smart quick
if you read read read
one of Brezhnev's books,
in a chair (anywhere)
in a chair (anywhere),
while a million comrades smile!

Hi ho, hi ho, we're reading Brezhnev's works,
we're loving volumes 1 through 8,
hi ho, hi ho, hi ho,
hi ho, hi ho, we haven't finished yet,
there're 7 volumes more – you bet!
Hi ho, hi ho, hi ho!

Hi ho! Hi ho!........Hi ho!

Andropov, champion of milk drinkers

(Composed on 6 and 8 April 2014)

Some say Andropov was already dead
when he was elected the communists' head –
we don't agree, we think that's a lie,
remember that he was the country's top spy,
and while supervising his network of spies,
he knew that deception involved a disguise.
Pretend to be ill, people think you are weak,
they pay less attention, while you work at your peak.

Sometimes, by day, he would rest in the clinic,
but please don't despair, please don't be a cynic.
Nighttime would come, he was out and about,
with false beard and moustache, just don't mind the gout.
He hung around bars, ordering milk –
drunkards and tipplers were not of his ilk,
but he felt he should tell them that drink to excess
is scarcely the road to health and success.

Rule, Chernenko!

(Composed on 5 April 2014. Does the refrain remind anyone else of "Rule, Britannia!"? Is it possible that one can sing the middle stanza to the fourth movement of Beethoven's Ninth Symphony?)

Rule, Chernenko! Chernenko rule the state,
though you came to office rather late.
Emphysema it seems it was your fate –
smoking cigarettes is not so great.

When Andropov, his predecessor,
took the vodka off the shelves.
Many Russians discontented
said they could not be themselves.
But Chernenko, he knew vodka
was as good as cigarettes:
put the bottles back in shops,
did it and had no regrets.

Rule, Chernenko! Chernenko rule the state,
though you came to office rather late.
Emphysema it seems it was your fate –
smoking cigarettes is not so great.

Perestroika (dance version)

(Inspired by the song "Collegiana", first recorded by Waring's Pennsylvanians in 1928; later revived by the Nitty Gritty Dirt Band. A few phrases here have been taken over directly from "Collegiana". Composed in April 2014.)

In the Kremlin they tried to stop him
from anything new or out of their view.
All of Russia was now in coma,
zastoj too was pretty near through.
Gorby'd found a new reformist hop,
reform 'til we drop,
we'll never stop.
If you wanna see, what is getting me
I'll show you how to do
perestroika, see how it's done,
make reforms, it's a lot of fun.
You add a bit of glasnost
and then you speed it up.

Comrade Ligachev never was glad
because of the migraine that he had,
but then came perestroika –
it never was a flop!

All good comrades and every communist
all hate the ominous – and how!
Two step new step, it's like a dance, you see –
but there will always be dead beats.
There was a coup, but it fell apart,
seems that the plotters weren't so smart.
Boris Yeltsin save the day – perestroika won!

Boris Yeltsin, you know it's Boris Yeltsin!

(Composed on 5 April 2014, on the couch, with the cat lying on my stomach. May be sung to the tune of "The Hunters of Kentucky", a top hit in the 18th century.)

Who is it whom the Russian people constantly are thanking?
Who is it who reformed the Russian mode of banking?
Who was it who gave oligarchs a little pow'r to veto
policies they didn't like? Don't you think that's neato?

Boris Yeltsin, you know it's Boris Yeltsin!
Boris Yeltsin, yes it was Boris Yeltsin!

And when he ran for president, he did some fancy dancing,
and when around the ladies, he could be so romancing,
and when it comes to alcohol, he knew he had no limit,
he belted out his campaign songs, he was never timid.

Boris Yeltsin, you know it's Boris Yeltsin!
Boris Yeltsin, yes it was Boris Yeltsin!

Putin on the moon

(Composed sometime between June 2007 and June 2010)

The US thinks they've won the race –
the first man on the moon –
but Putin knows that outer space
can play to Moscow's tune.

No head of state has gone to Mars
or through the Milky Way
but Putin plans to see the stars
and put on a display.

The public has a gnawing thirst
for something new and more;
so Putin plans to be the first
as head of state to soar

To distant stars and planets
and circle 'round the sun,
intent to show the world below
that Russia's number one.

But Putin's ship is thrown off course
because it launched too soon,
and Russia's leader finds he's forced
to settle for the moon.

He finds the stars and stripes are there
and hurls it to the ground,
and plants a Russian flag instead,
then starts to look around.

Putin now comes on the air,
the Russians ought to know:
Aside from him the moon is bare,
there's no place here to go.

"So if you want a party,
you're better off at home,"
he tells his people honestly,
"'cause here you're all alone."

But weightlessness is kinda cool,
so Putin leaps and skips,
before he packs his bag and leaves
to fly back on his ship.

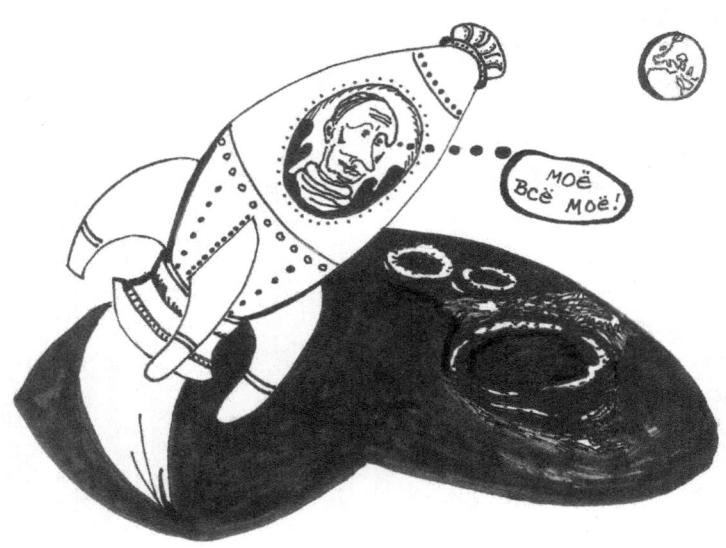

Solipsists for Putin

(Composed on 9 April 2014; minor modifications on 10 and 11 April 2014)

As a wise old solipsist, I know you don't exist,
and nor does Mr. Putin, if you must insist.
The whole world's an illusion, dancing in my mind –
that's why I've formed a union to hang out with my kind.
My friends are also solipsists, who don't think I exist,
and when it comes to politics, we usually resist
temptations to engage ourselves – we cannot see the reason
why we should spend time with it, when the whole world's an illusion.
But though we are all solipsists, you'll find that we are rootin'
for the Russian president, one Mister Vlado Putin.
Since he's just a figment of my mind's creation,
I can change our Mr. Putin by sheer imagination.
So now I'm thinking really hard that in my latest snore,
Putin is a singer with talent, yes, galore,
and when he belts out "Blueberry Hill", I dream the crowd's ecstatic:
they clap, they cheer, they shout his name – he might be hypostatic.

Putin fantasizes

(Composed on 13 April 2014)

Eastern Ukraine – isn't it plain? That should be Russian once again.
Kazakhstan, why that is next! Then we'll proceed to mop up the rest.
Latvia – well, that's a maybe, member of NATO but just a baby;
it's so small, the West won't miss it – if they do, well, they can piss it.
Russians also in LA, we'll liberate them too, some day.
Raise my glass and pour a jigger, Russia just keeps growing bigger.

SOVIET FRIENDS ABROAD

Well hello, Zhivkov

(May be sung to the tune of "Hello Dolly"; composed on 6 and 9 September 2010)

Well hello, Zhivkov,
it's so nice, Zhivkov,
to see the posters with your smiling face.
You're looking wise, Zhivkov,
and your eyes, Zhivkov,
follow me as I go to another place.

Well yes, *you* know, Zhivkov,
where we go, Zhivkov,
in meeting all our goals within the plan!
So, Comrade Zhivkov, you are
such a supernova,
count me as your most obedient fan!

Well well, hello, Comrade,
lucky us, Comrade,
that all your children are so bright and strong,
you gave them posts, Zhivkov,
it's them I toast, Zhivkov,
it's nice to have you back where you belong (with us).

You changed the names, Comrade,
of men and dames, Comrade,
to sound more Slavic than they were before,
So – Comrade, you've always been a star,
Comrade, you've always been a star,
Comrade, you've always been a shining star.

Enver, don't shoot

(Inspired by a Yugoslav joke circulating at the time that Mehmet Shehu was reported to have killed himself; there were three competing versions of the event, all replicated here. Composed sometime between June 2007 and June 2010)

Enver Hoxha – he knew French,
he had the best seat on the bench.
He knew Shehu from the start,
abolished taxes: that was smart,
built some bunkers 'cross the land,
half a million – that was grand.
All the while he thought he knew
that Mehmet Shehu would be true.

Mehmet Shehu was a hoot!
His last words were "Enver don't shoot!"
As he loaded up his gun,
He shouted "There's just one number one."
"Enver, don't shoot! Enver, don't shoot!"
His last words were "Enver, don't shoot!"

Shehu was prime minister,
some said that he was sinister.
He was tough – now that's for sure,
For his foes, death was the cure.
Skanderbeg had a "giant mind"
or so he revealed to humankind.
Mao Zedong inspired him,
but the Little Red Book – it tired him.

Mehmet Shehu was a hoot!
His last words were "Enver don't shoot!"
As he loaded up his gun,
He shouted "There's just one number one."

"Enver, don't shoot! Enver, don't shoot!"
His last words were "Enver, don't shoot!"

Then they quarreled and they split,
Enver Hoxha threw a fit.
And when he needed a problem solver,
he just reached for his revolver.
"Mehmet Shehu, you've betrayed
the party and it's time you paid
for your independent point of view.
Now it's time to say adieu."

Mehmet Shehu was a hoot!
His last words were "Enver don't shoot!"
As he loaded up his gun,
He shouted "There's just one number one."
"Enver, don't shoot! Enver, don't shoot!"
His last words were "Enver, don't shoot!"

Enver Hoxha had decided
Shehu would be "suicided"
Shehu left a little note,
Said it was an accident and I quote,
"I cleaned my gun and took a breath,
and then it went off and caused my death."
Or maybe it was suicide,
plain and simple: you decide.

Mehmet Shehu was a hoot!
His last words were "Enver don't shoot!"
As he loaded up his gun,
He shouted "There's just one number one."
"Enver, don't shoot! Enver, don't shoot!"
His last words were "Enver, don't shoot!"

The golden words of Mao Zedong

(May be sung to the tune of "The yellow rose of Texas"; composed sometime between June 2007 and June 2010)

I was re-educated in the time of Mao Zedong,
I memorized his Red Book and read it all day long,
Although I had a Ph.D. I worked down in a mine,
the labor helped me realize that China had it fine.

Oh the golden words of Mao Zedong are all I need to know,
they fill my life, enrich my mind and make me smile and glow,
and though it's sure that much has changed, there's much that's stayed the same,
and here I'd like to mention the chairman's well-earned fame.

A hundred flowers tried to bloom but they were mostly weeds,
there was nothing good about them – not what the country needs,
We used to have mass meetings, down in the village square,
we rounded up the landlords and explained what was unfair.

We brought out some reformers and made them wear dunce caps
and admit that their experiments had resulted in mishaps,
we had a revolution and changed the names of streets,
we dressed alike and sang good songs and managed many feats.

Oh the golden words of Mao Zedong are all I need to know,
they fill my life, enrich my mind and make me smile and glow,
and though it's sure that much has changed, there's much that's stayed the same,
and here I'd like to mention the chairman's well-earned fame.

让哲学变为群众手里的尖锐武器

Die gute Zeiten rollen lassen

(Verse written (sometime between June 2007 and June 2010) to recall that Otto Grotewohl was chairman of the Council of Ministers from 1949 to 1964 in the East German SED, as the communist party was called, and that local East Germans would raise their glasses of wine, in his time, with a toast, "Zum Wohl, zum Grotewohl!", meaning "To your health, to Grotewohl!, a pun on his name. In an unrelated allusion, the verse recalls that the Vikings reckoned their tax in quantities of butter.)

Hier in Leipzig vi like relax
vi like pretend vi don't pay tax,
vi pull down pants und bare our asses,
den vi raise up high our glasses
und vi shout out loud und clear:
"Ja, vi like it living hier
in our socialistic land
und singing mit de marching band.
Sure, let the good times roll,
die gute Zeiten rollen lassen!"

Tax man makes heads spin und flutter
but vi tell, "Vi pay with butter.
Vi have buckets, vi drive Wagen,
how much butter is you magen?
We're not Vikings but vi like
wenn de taxes do not hike.
Ja, vi like it living hier
in our socialistic land
und singing mit de marching band.
Sure, let the good times roll,
die gute Zeiten rollen lassen!"

Come and see our waterfall,
raise your glass and say "Zum Wohl!"
Venn you've drunk a couple glass
then you say "Zum Grotewohl!"

but you know the party's right,
this seems certain venn you're tight,
When you ready now you say
"Ich trink' zur ganzen SED!"
Now we've had some alcohol,
ja zum Wohl und Grotewohl!
Best it's time for lemon frenzy
squeeze the juice into your tea
spoon in honey, stir and sip,
just leave bisschen yet for me.

Ceausescu's monkeys

(Composed sometime between 1997 and 2003)

'Twas the night before May Day
and all through the land
Not a comrade was stirring –
that's how it was planned.
The self-criticisms were laid
on the desktop with care,
in hopes that Ceausescu
soon would be there.
But old Nick was soaring up high in the sky
his sleigh being pulled by a bevy of monkeys.
"Come Voitec, come Trofim, come Cornel Burtica,
Come Gheorghe Petrescu, come all of my flunkeys!"
I sat on my bed and heard such a commotion,
I figured it must be a purge or demotion.
And then there he was, that jolly old elf,
dressed in Bolshevik red, in spite of himself.
He unpacked his five-year plans right under my eye,
and then sprang up the chimney and took to the sky.
And as he flew by, I heard him exclaim,
"Whatever goes wrong, I don't take the blame."

Husak's duck

(Composed sometime between 1997 and 2003)

Sing a son of Husak, a pocket full of plans,
Four and twenty dailies, finished off by bans.
When the bans were lifted, the dailies began to sing:
Now wasn't that a reactionary dish to set before the king.
The censor was in the garden, checking the party line.
The planner was in the parlour with the economy in decline.
And Husak was in the throne room, fondling his duck,
While all around his ministers let things run amok.

The duck had lots to say, of course, like quack and quack and quack,
but that was just as good as what he got from party hacks.
One day dear Comrade Husak was purging all his foes
when along came his duck-friend and pecked off his nose.

Ulbricht's hamsters

(Composed sometime between 1997 and 2003)

"How pretty your little cage is,
my little hamster friends,"
said Walter Ulbricht,
General Secretary of the SED,
to his pet hamsters.
"The bars are nice and firm,
they will protect you
from the world.
But please,
my pretty pets,
don't get too close to them,
because I have electrified
the bars.
I think the effect
would quite surprise you.
But how nice it is
inside your cage
with lots of toys
and ferris wheels.
You have it good,
my lucky pets –
much better than hamsters
in capitalistic systems."

Mao's cockroach

(Composed sometime between 1997 and 2003)

Mao Zedong
Great Leader of the Chinese people
Banned all pets!
Cultural Revolution,
he called it:
the Great Proletarian Cultural Revolution.

"Close the theaters, close the schools,
close the temples,
ban all operas (except "High Tide of Revolutionary Fervor" and
"The party – the people – a better future"),
ban all pets!
Ban all films (except for agitprop)
Long live the Working People of China!"

Mao didn't like pets.
But every night
when he went to the fridge for milk,
a small cockroach ran under the counter
a small cockroach Mao called "October,"
after the Great October Revolution.
October didn't like the light,
He liked it dark,
He kept out of sight
during the day.
Communism, capitalism – they all seemed the same,
thought October.
No matter what the system,
if you don't watch out,
somebody will step on you.

Ho Chi Minh's "Parakeet"

(Composed sometime between 1998 and 2004)

Ho Chi Minh of Vietnam
always stayed so nice and calm
You could bring him troubling news,
he would never get the blues.
Even when his troops were beat,
he'd just stroke his parakeet.
"Squawk! Victory to the toiling masses!
Victory to the toiling masses!"
His parakeet was right on cue
Helping Ho to make it through,
But then it came to Ho Chi Minh --
a revelation on the chin:
Parakeets don't like such talk,
they shouldn't even like to squawk.
Just whistle idle bourgeois tunes,
no rousing slogans for his platoons.
"Squawk! All hail the proletarian masses!
Onward to proletarian revolution!"
The leader called his adjutant
and told him over claret,
"This parakeet, she is a fraud.
Let's hang her from the garret.
A parrot that is what she is,
engaged in masquerade."
But the parrot looked him in the eye,
showed no sign of being afraid.
"Squawk! Long live Marx and Lenin
and the people's leader, Ho Chi Minh!"
And Ho Chi Minh then realized

that this parrot was a red,
and could be much more useful living,
than as a martyr -- dead.
And so they stayed together,
this parrot and her feeder:
a proletarian pseudo-parakeet,
and the people's leader.

Castro's speeches and his Chihuaha's comment

(Composed sometime between 1998 and 2004)

The people of Havana were so happy,
they cheered their leader.
They were happy, for his speech
had lasted just four hours --
not the usual six or seven.
They had stood under the bright hot sun
for just four hours,
because their leader had been succinct,
unusually succinct.
But one thing was the same
that day:
Fidel's Chihuahua kept trying to interrupt the Cuban presidente,
"Arp! Arp!" the chihuahua barked
It pawed Fidel's pants and barked,
"Arp! Arp!"
Comrade, you must wait 'til I have finished,"
Castro said to his chihuahua
but Comrade kept up the fuss.
It had always been that way --
for thirty years.
Si, it was that way for thirty years:
when el Presidente
addressed the Cuban masses,
Comrade would begin
to shout "Arp! Arp!"
But then, one fine day --
or perhaps it was not fine at all,
but who can remember *that* any longer? --
Castro said to himself,

"My dog's not saying 'arp, arp' at all.
In contrario, he is an art lover,
and has been telling me, 'Art, Art!'"
And from that day onward, presidente
heeding his Comrade's call,
included long discussions of Van Gogh, Renoir, and Monet
in all his perorations.
And there was now so much to say,
Fidel now would talk for nine
inspired by a sense of the sublime,
devoting all his hours to art,
Trying to make up for lost time.
He owed all this to Comrade,
a canine friend of art,
who'd proved beyond the slightest doubt,
that painting warms the heart.

Kim Il Sung's fellow traveler

(Composed sometime between 1998 and 2005)

"No city is complete
without a giant gold statue of me,"
Kim il Sung once said
and he was right.
He put one up in P'yongyang --
that was a complete city.
It stood 300 feet in height,
from base to crown.
But few have noticed
that, under his golden arm,
the Great Noble Leader --
gold version --
is holding a small crocodile,
his fellow traveler.
Kim often said
that crocodiles were "forward-looking"
And he was right.
But there was more:
"Many persons will travel with us
along much of the path to communism,"
Kim il Sung once said,
echoing Stalin,
and he was right.
"They can be useful,
even if they will not travel with us
the whole distance."
And he was right.
A crocodile may not know much
about communism,

but he may be useful
all the same.
Kim Il Sung once said so,
or something to that effect;
it does not really matter exactly what he said,
what matters
is that he was right.
And I agree with him --
whatever he said,
because he was right.
His crocodile was less profound
And talked mainly about the menu.
He claimed that fish and birds and turtles
were the most flavorful,
And he was right.

Tito and his self-managing goat

(Composed sometime between 1997 and 2004)

Tito had a fancy car and he had a fancy coat
And he had some fancy notions that he shared with his goat.
His goat's name was Hector and Hector liked to hear
About the workers' councils that had started to appear.

Tito told him *all* about these councils' operations,
About the friendly harmony between the country's nations.
The goat became so curious that it's said he started lurking
Around the council chambers to see the system working.

The goat was very clever and donned a smart disguise
And no one recognized him, not even UDBa's spies.
But thus disguised the goat was seated at the council meeting
Even though his attention span was really very fleeting.

Now treated as a communist, this sneaky goat was asked
To carry out some functions and accomplish certain tasks.
The goat became the chairgoat in charge of a commission
To analyze the causes of the budget's fast attrition.

Now as clever as this quadriped appeared to all concerned
And as much as he had studied and as much as he had learned,
These fiscal complications were not at all his game.
So he delegated duties to a man of little fame.

But the goat was somewhat skeptical that this man could work alone,
And so he had him followed and he bugged his telephone.
But all he proved conclusively was that this man was lazy
And that everything he spoke or wrote was impenetrably hazy.

The date arrived on which the goat's report was coming due
But the man of little fame and his bureaucratic crew
Had not accomplished anything, leaving Hector in the lurch.
So Hector launched a campaign against the Christian Church.

"Reports -- they matter little in this period of stress.
We must combat our enemies, and cope with this duress,"
So said this Comrade Hector, hoping to create
Confusion so that people would forget that he was late.

The campaign gathered lots of steam and everyone joined in,
Even Comrade Tito lent his tenor to the din.
The goat was hailed and decorated and in the common parlance,
Was said to be the Yugoslav Self-Manager par excellence.

In time a careful porcupine drafted the report,
Which repeated all the usual phrases, offering no retort,
And affixed goat Hector's signature so it might be supposed,
That this raw assessment had by Hector been composed.

The goat went on to other tasks, handling them with skill
And stoking up new campaigns whenever things went ill.
Eventually the goat retired and no longer made the news,
And devoted his remaining days to giving interviews.

Even now when people talk of Tito and his time,
They still remember what was lovely and sublime.
People rarely talk these days of Tito's pants or coat
But everyone still talks about his Self-Managing Goat.

Kadar's pedigree Pooch

(Composed sometime between 1997 and 2004)

He loved to go for a walk by day,
He loved to chat with ordinary folk.
That Janós Kádár dressed so simply,
Without so much as a cloak.
He took in the town with a grin on his face
And a pedigree pooch on his shoulder.
The townfolk were a bit wary at first
But gradually became a bit bolder.

"Comrade Kádár, good morning, and how's your pooch today,
And how's our glorious leader?"
"Your leader is doing fine and the pooch is quite sublime.
We're just off to visit her breeder.
She suffers from terrible nightmares
Of show trials and purges and camps.
I've told her that that was Rakósi,
That her nightmares bear the stamp

Of an age that is bygone and finished,
Of an age that was blacker than black."
But she shudders and winces regardless,
Lest Rakósi's Bolshies come back.
Nowadays it's hard to remember
Why some called him "Janós the Mild".
But no one in Hungary will ever forget
How he treated his pooch like his child.

Riding high with Enver Hoxha

(Composed sometime between 1997 and 2004)

I'm feeling on top of the world,
whenever I remember,
the time I spent with the glorious leader
one October and November.

Comrade Hoxha, Comrade Hoxha, you fought the capitalist beast,
I've often heard the older folk recall you liked to say
that capitalists were just like sheep – both needed to be fleeced
if Albania was to go the communistic way.

You wouldn't let the sport fans cheer – it was 'undignified',
you wouldn't let a band play rock 'n' roll,
People sure could praise the party, and sing about their pride,
But in music you would always keep control.

I'm feeling on top of the world
whenever I remember
the time I spent with the glorious leader
one October and November.

I volunteered to do my part in the people's work brigade,
we camped outside and helped to pave a street,
I saw the people's mascot sheep marching in the shade.
While we toiled beneath the sun I heard them bleat:

Ba-ba, said the sheep, and sang the system's praises
And learned the sounds that the agents came to teach,
Each sheep's grateful for the party's wisdom and grateful when it grazes
And grateful for the leader's latest speech.

I was a happy comrade, until I got some doubts,
But then I fled and I got out,
leaving Hoxha's sheep to sit and pout.
Hey communists, you think you know
that purging can be fun,
That seems progressive for a while,
until you are the one,
who's put on trial for saying things
'bout what the sheep are doing,
Don't tell me, please, I'd rather not
be mixed up in what's brewing.
Hey party people, I like sheep,
but not as much as you do,
And most of what your speeches say
sounds like so much voo-doo.

Gomulka's Aardvark

(Composed in early 2006)

Your aardvark may not need much meat, but we do, Gomulka!
We're not vegetarians: So go, go, Gomulka!

You let your aardvark ham it up
and help you with the plan,
You tell him how you see through jokes:
you must be superman!

You tell your aardvark how you once
defied the Kremlin's bosses,
They had to take you on your terms,
you made them count their losses.

Your aardvark may not need much meat, but we do, Gomulka!
We're not vegetarians: So go, go, Gomulka!

Your aardvark wants to suck some ants,
the people want to eat,
The ants are free in Poland
but you raise the price of meat!

The Poles believe Your Comradeship
could use a long vacation,
So you step down and take a bow
to cheers and huge ovation.

Your aardvark may not need much meat, but we do, Gomulka!
We're not vegetarians: So go, go, Gomulka!

Gierek the leader & Melsor the toad

(Composed after a short visit to Slovenia in November 2004. This ditty may be sung to the tune of "A Pub With No Beer".)

Ed Gierek was Polish and so was his toad,
to whom he'd composed a magnificent ode.
When Melsor the toad wished to hear a good tune,
the Great Edvard Gierek would commence to croon:

Refrain:
"We'll raise high the wages and keep prices low,
we'll borrow the difference and pay as we go
'Cause the people want trabants to drive out to view
their socialist comrades all lined in a queue."

The heroes of socialist labor all toiled
to assure that the Five Year Plan wouldn't be spoiled,
And the communist leaders who had nothing to gain
would smile to their comrades and intoned this refrain:

Refrain:
"We'll raise high the wages and keep prices low,
we'll borrow the difference and pay as we go
'Cause the people want trabants to drive out to view
their socialist comrades all lined in a queue."

To purchase the foods that they wanted to eat
the comrades would queue up right in the street,
The shops opened at ten but you shouldn't be late,
so get in the queue before half past eight:

Refrain:
"We'll raise high the wages and keep prices low,
we'll borrow the difference and pay as we go,
'Cause the people want toilets to take in the view
of comrades outside lining up in a queue."

www.ingramcontent.com/pod-product-compliance
Lightning Source LLC
Chambersburg PA
CBHW032302150426
43195CB00008BA/551